CONTENTS

INTRODUCTION TO QUICKBOOKS ONLINE

Understanding the Importance of Accounting for Small Businesses

1.1.1 The Role of Accounting in Business Success

Accounting plays a pivotal role in determining the success of any business. It serves as the language of financial transactions, providing a systematic way to record, analyze, and interpret financial information. The fundamental purpose of accounting is to enable businesses to make informed decisions based on their financial health and performance. It involves the recording of all financial activities, including revenue generation, expenses, and assets. By maintaining accurate and up-to-date financial records, businesses gain insight into their profitability, liquidity, and overall financial stability.

Financial Decision-Making: One of the primary functions of accounting is to support decision-making processes within a business. Managers rely on financial statements such as income statements, balance sheets, and cash flow statements to assess the company's financial position. This information helps in identifying areas that need improvement, formulating budgets, and setting strategic goals. Effective financial decision-making, guided by accounting principles, ensures that resources are allocated efficiently, leading to business growth and sustainability.

Compliance and Regulation: Accounting also plays a crucial role in ensuring that businesses adhere to legal and regulatory requirements. Various accounting standards and frameworks, such as Generally Accepted Accounting Principles (GAAP) or International Financial Reporting Standards (IFRS), dictate how financial information should be recorded and presented. Compliance with these standards is not only essential for legal reasons but also builds trust among stakeholders, including investors, creditors, and regulatory bodies.

Performance Evaluation: Business success is often measured through the lens of financial performance. Accounting facilitates the evaluation of a company's profitability, efficiency, and overall effectiveness. Ratios and financial indicators derived from accounting data allow businesses to compare their performance over time, against industry benchmarks, and with competitors. This performance evaluation is instrumental in identifying strengths, weaknesses, opportunities, and threats, helping businesses refine their strategies for sustained success.

Investor Confidence: Investors, whether they are shareholders or potential financiers, rely on accurate and transparent financial information to assess the viability of an investment. Through financial reports, accounting provides a snapshot of a company's financial health, enabling investors to make informed decisions. Strong and transparent financial reporting builds confidence among investors, attracting capital that is vital for expansion, innovation, and overall business growth.

Tax Planning and Compliance: Accounting is indispensable in the realm of tax planning and compliance. Proper accounting practices ensure that businesses accurately calculate and fulfill their tax obligations. By keeping meticulous records of income, expenses, and deductions, businesses can optimize their tax positions and avoid legal issues. Understanding tax implications is crucial for strategic planning and ensuring that a business remains financially resilient in the face of changing tax regulations.

In conclusion, the role of accounting in business success is multifaceted. It goes beyond mere bookkeeping to provide a comprehensive understanding of a company's financial landscape. From aiding in decision-making to ensuring compliance and fostering investor confidence, accounting is an integral aspect of achieving and sustaining success in the dynamic world of business.

1.1.2 Common Financial Challenges for Small Business Owners

Small business owners face a unique set of financial challenges that can significantly impact their ability to thrive in a competitive market. While these challenges may vary across industries, several common financial hurdles are pervasive among small enterprises. Understanding and effectively addressing these challenges are crucial for the financial stability and long-term success of small businesses.

Cash Flow Management: One of the most common

financial challenges for small business owners is managing cash flow. Uneven cash flow, resulting from delayed payments or seasonal fluctuations, can disrupt day-to-day operations and hinder growth. To address this, small business owners need to implement effective cash flow management strategies, such as invoicing promptly, negotiating favorable payment terms with suppliers, and maintaining a cash reserve for emergencies.

Limited Access to Capital: Small businesses often struggle to access the capital necessary for expansion, equipment purchase, or even day-to-day operations. Traditional lenders may perceive small businesses as riskier investments, making it challenging to secure loans. To overcome this challenge, entrepreneurs can explore alternative financing options such as crowdfunding, peer-to-peer lending, or government-backed loan programs designed to support small businesses.

Budget Constraints: Setting and sticking to a budget is a constant challenge for small business owners, who must carefully allocate resources to various operational needs. Limited budgets can impact marketing efforts, employee salaries, and technology investments. Successful small business owners prioritize budgeting, focusing on essential expenses while identifying areas for cost savings and efficiency improvements.

Regulatory Compliance: Navigating complex regulatory requirements poses a significant challenge for small businesses. Compliance with tax laws, employment regulations, and industry-specific standards demands time and resources that may strain a small business's financial capacity. Seeking professional advice, staying informed about regulatory changes, and implementing robust internal controls can help small businesses maintain compliance without incurring unnecessary costs.

Technology Adoption Costs: In an increasingly digital business environment, small businesses face the challenge of adopting and integrating new technologies. While technology can enhance efficiency and competitiveness, the upfront costs of implementation and staff training can strain limited budgets. Small business owners must carefully evaluate the return on investment (ROI) of technology solutions and prioritize those that offer the most significant impact on their operations.

Market Competition and Pricing Pressures: Competing with larger corporations and navigating pricing pressures in the market is a perpetual challenge for small businesses. Price wars and discounting strategies employed by larger competitors can squeeze profit margins. Small business owners must focus on differentiating their products or services, providing exceptional customer service, and building strong relationships within their niche to withstand pricing pressures.

1.1.3 How QuickBooks Online Addresses Financial Management Needs

QuickBooks Online (QBO) has emerged as a powerful and popular tool for addressing the financial management needs of businesses, especially small and medium-sized enterprises. This cloud-based accounting software offers a range of features designed to streamline financial processes, enhance accuracy, and provide valuable insights into a company's financial health. Let's explore how QuickBooks Online addresses various financial management needs.

Bookkeeping and Accounting Automation: QuickBooks Online simplifies bookkeeping and accounting tasks by automating many processes. It allows users to connect bank and credit card accounts, automatically categorizing transactions and reconciling accounts. This automation not only saves time but also reduces the risk of errors associated with manual data entry.

Real-Time Financial Reporting: One of the standout features of QuickBooks Online is its ability to generate real-time financial reports. Users can access up-to-date income statements, balance sheets, and cash flow statements, providing a clear and current snapshot of the company's financial position. This real-time reporting capability is invaluable for informed decision-making and strategic planning.

Invoicing and Payment Processing: QuickBooks Online streamlines the invoicing process, allowing businesses to create and send professional invoices to clients. The software also facilitates online payment processing, enabling businesses to get paid faster. Integrations with various payment gateways make it easy for customers to settle invoices electronically, reducing the hassle of manual payment handling.

Expense Tracking and Management: Tracking expenses is a critical aspect of financial management, and QuickBooks Online simplifies this process. Users can easily capture and categorize expenses, attach receipts digitally, and monitor spending patterns. The software provides insights into where the money is going, aiding in budgeting and cost control efforts.

Payroll Processing: QuickBooks Online offers integrated payroll processing features, allowing businesses to manage employee salaries, tax withholdings, and compliance seamlessly. This simplifies the often complex and time-consuming task of payroll administration, ensuring accuracy and compliance with tax regulations.

Integration with Third-Party Apps: To cater to diverse business needs, QuickBooks Online offers integrations with a wide array of third-party applications. These integrations cover areas such as inventory management, customer relationship management (CRM), e-commerce, and more. This flexibility allows businesses to tailor their financial management processes to suit their specific requirements.

Cloud-Based Accessibility: Being a cloud-based solution, QuickBooks Online provides anytime, anywhere access to financial data. Users can log in from various devices, facilitating collaboration among team members and enabling remote work. The cloud-based nature of QBO also ensures that data is securely backed up and accessible even in the event of hardware failures.

Scalability and Affordability: QuickBooks Online offers different subscription plans, making it scalable to accommodate the needs of businesses of varying sizes. Whether a startup or an established enterprise, businesses can choose a plan that aligns with their requirements and budget constraints. This scalability ensures that businesses can continue using QuickBooks Online as they grow.

In conclusion, QuickBooks Online addresses a wide range of financial management needs by providing automated bookkeeping, real-time reporting, streamlined invoicing and payment processing, expense tracking, payroll management, integration with third-party apps, cloud-based accessibility, and scalability. Small and medium-sized businesses can leverage these features to enhance efficiency, accuracy, and overall financial control.

Overview Of Quickbooks Online Features

1.2.1 Cloud-Based Accounting Advantages of QuickBooks Online

Cloud-based accounting has revolutionized the way businesses manage their financial data, and QuickBooks Online stands at the forefront of this transformation. The advantages of QuickBooks Online (QBO) as a cloud-based accounting solution are manifold, catering to the evolving needs of modern businesses.

Real-Time Accessibility: One of the standout features of QuickBooks Online is its real-time accessibility. Users can access their financial data anytime, anywhere, provided they have an internet connection. This flexibility empowers business owners and accountants to stay connected with their financial information on the go, facilitating timely decision-making.

Automatic Updates: Unlike traditional accounting software that requires manual updates, QuickBooks Online operates on a cloud-based infrastructure, enabling automatic updates. This ensures that users always have the latest features, bug fixes, and compliance updates without the hassle of downloading and installing patches.

Cost-Effective Scalability: QuickBooks Online offers

scalable plans, allowing businesses to choose a subscription that aligns with their current needs and budget. As a company grows, it can easily upgrade to a more advanced plan without the need for significant infrastructure changes. This scalability makes QBO an attractive option for startups and small businesses aiming for controlled expenditure.

Collaborative Working Environment: QuickBooks Online facilitates seamless collaboration among team members, accountants, and other stakeholders. Multiple users can simultaneously access and work on the same set of financial data, enhancing efficiency and reducing the delays associated with traditional accounting methods.

Integration Capabilities: QBO boasts a wide range of integrations with other business tools and applications. This integration capability allows businesses to streamline their workflow by connecting QuickBooks Online with services like payment gateways, e-commerce platforms, and expense management tools. This interconnected ecosystem minimizes data silos and enhances overall operational efficiency.

Enhanced Reporting and Analytics: Cloud-based accounting, particularly in QuickBooks Online, provides robust reporting and analytics features. Users can generate customized reports, track key performance indicators, and gain valuable insights into their financial health. This data-driven approach empowers businesses to make informed decisions and adapt to changing market conditions.

Automatic Data Backup: QuickBooks Online automatically backs up financial data to secure cloud servers. This feature eliminates the risk of data loss due to hardware failures, accidents, or other unforeseen events. The peace of mind that comes with knowing that critical financial information is securely stored in the cloud is invaluable for businesses aiming to minimize operational disruptions.

Compliance and Security: QBO prioritizes data security and compliance with industry standards. The cloud infrastructure undergoes regular security audits and updates, ensuring that sensitive financial information remains protected against cyber threats. This commitment to security is particularly crucial in an era where data breaches pose a significant risk to businesses of all sizes.

1.2.2 Accessibility and Multi-User Collaboration in QuickBooks Online

QuickBooks Online (QBO) not only excels in providing accessibility to financial data but also fosters a collaborative working environment through its multi-user capabilities. These features play a pivotal role in enhancing efficiency, communication, and overall productivity within businesses.

Remote Accessibility: The cloud-based nature of QuickBooks Online allows users to access their accounting data remotely. Whether working from home, during travel, or at client meetings, users can log in to QBO from any device with internet connectivity. This flexibility is especially beneficial for businesses with remote or geographically dispersed teams.

Multi-User Collaboration: QuickBooks Online's multi-user collaboration feature facilitates concurrent access to the same set of financial data by multiple users. This capability is invaluable in collaborative work environments where various team members, including accountants and financial advisors, need simultaneous access. Real-time collaboration reduces delays, minimizes errors, and enhances communication within the financial team.

User Permissions and Controls: To maintain data integrity and security, QuickBooks Online allows administrators to set user permissions and controls. This feature ensures that each team member has access only to the relevant sections of the financial data based on their role and responsibilities. For example, a sales manager may have access to sales-related data without viewing sensitive payroll information.

Audit Trail Functionality: In a multi-user environment, tracking changes to financial data is crucial for transparency and accountability. QuickBooks Online includes an audit trail functionality that records every transaction, modification, or deletion made by users. This detailed audit trail enhances the ability to trace any discrepancies, fostering a culture of accountability within the organization.

Communication within the Platform: QBO integrates communication tools within the platform, allowing users to leave comments, notes, or questions directly on specific transactions. This built-in communication feature streamlines collaboration by providing a centralized space for discussions related to financial data. This is especially helpful in resolving queries, clarifying transaction details, and ensuring a smooth workflow.

Real-Time Updates: Multi-user collaboration in QuickBooks Online extends to real-time updates. When one user makes changes to financial data, those changes are immediately reflected for other authorized users. This instantaneous synchronization eliminates the need for manual data consolidation and reduces the risk of working with outdated information.

Training and Support for Users: QuickBooks Online recognizes the importance of user proficiency in leveraging its collaborative features. The platform offers training resources and customer support to help users understand the multi-user functionalities effectively. This commitment to user education ensures that businesses can make the most of the collaborative tools provided by QBO.

In essence, QuickBooks Online goes beyond providing remote accessibility; it creates a collaborative ecosystem where team members can work seamlessly together. The platform's multi-user capabilities, user permissions, audit trail functionality, communication tools, real-time updates, and dedicated support contribute to a dynamic and efficient financial workflow.

1.2.3 Security and Data Backup in QuickBooks Online

Security and data backup are paramount considerations in any accounting system, and QuickBooks Online (QBO) addresses these concerns with a robust approach. The platform employs advanced security measures and automatic data backup mechanisms to safeguard sensitive financial information.

Secure Cloud Infrastructure: QuickBooks Online operates on a secure cloud infrastructure, utilizing encryption protocols to protect data during transmission and storage. This ensures that financial information remains confidential and guarded against unauthorized access. The platform's commitment to a secure cloud environment is crucial in an era where cyber threats are constantly evolving.

Authentication and Access Controls: QBO prioritizes user authentication and access controls to prevent unauthorized access to financial data. Multi-factor authentication adds an extra layer of security by requiring users to verify their identity through multiple means. Additionally, the platform allows administrators to set granular access controls, ensuring that only authorized personnel can view or modify specific financial information.

Regular Security Audits and Updates: To stay ahead of potential security threats, QuickBooks Online undergoes regular security audits and updates. These measures ensure that the platform adheres to the latest security standards and patches any vulnerabilities promptly. This proactive approach is essential in safeguarding against emerging cyber threats and ensuring the integrity of financial data.

Automatic Data Backup: QuickBooks Online's automatic data backup feature provides a failsafe against data loss. The platform routinely backs up financial data to secure cloud servers, mitigating the risks associated with hardware failures, accidents, or unforeseen events. This automated backup process eliminates the need for manual intervention, reducing the likelihood of data loss due to human error.

Data Recovery Options: In the event of data loss or corruption, QuickBooks Online offers data recovery options. Users can restore their data to a previous point in time, ensuring that they can recover critical financial information with minimal disruption. This feature provides businesses with a safety net, allowing them to quickly recover from unforeseen data-related incidents.

Secure Data Transmission: When users access QuickBooks Online from different devices and locations, the platform ensures the security of data transmission. Encrypted connections protect the information exchanged between the user's device and the cloud servers, mitigating the risk of data interception or tampering. This focus on secure data transmission enhances the overall safety of using QBO in various working environments.

Compliance with Industry Standards: QuickBooks Online aligns with industry standards and regulations related to data security and privacy. This commitment to compliance ensures that businesses using the platform adhere to legal requirements, providing an additional layer of assurance for users concerned about regulatory compliance.

User Education on Security Best Practices: Recognizing the role of users in maintaining a secure environment, QuickBooks Online offers educational resources on security best practices. This includes guidance on creating strong passwords, recognizing phishing attempts, and ensuring the security of login credentials. User education is a proactive measure to enhance the overall security posture of businesses using QBO.

Up Your Quickbooks Online Account

1.3.1 Creating a New Account on QuickBooks Online

Creating a new account on QuickBooks Online (QBO) is a straightforward process that is integral to the efficient management of your business finances. QuickBooks Online is a cloud-based accounting solution that allows users to access their financial data from anywhere with an internet connection. To create a new account, start by visiting the QuickBooks Online website and selecting the "Sign Up" or "Try it free" option.

Upon selecting the sign-up option, you will be prompted to enter your email address and create a password. Ensure that the password is secure and complies with QuickBooks' security standards. After providing these initial details, you will need to input your business information, such as the business name, type, and industry. This step helps QuickBooks tailor its features to your specific business needs.

As part of the account creation process, you may also be required to add your business banking details. QuickBooks Online streamlines financial management by syncing with your bank accounts, allowing for automatic transaction updates and categorization. This feature enhances accuracy and saves time by reducing manual data entry.

Once you've completed these steps, QuickBooks will guide you through the initial setup, including adding your products or services, customers, and vendors. This process lays the foundation for efficient bookkeeping and financial tracking within the platform.

Key Points:

1. Start by visiting the QuickBooks Online website and selecting the "Sign Up" or "Try it free" option.

2. Provide basic information about your business, such as name, type, and industry.

3. Input your business banking details for seamless synchronization with QuickBooks.

4. Follow the guided setup process to add products or services, customers, and vendors.

1.3.2 Choosing the Right QuickBooks Online Subscription

Plan

Selecting the appropriate QuickBooks Online subscription plan is crucial to maximizing the platform's benefits while managing costs effectively. QuickBooks offers various subscription plans, each catering to different business needs. Choosing the right plan depends on factors such as the size of your business, the complexity of your financial operations, and your budget.

QuickBooks Online typically offers plans like Simple Start, Essentials, and Plus. The Simple Start plan is suitable for small businesses with basic accounting needs, while the Essentials plan includes additional features like bill management and time tracking. The Plus plan offers advanced functionalities such as inventory tracking and project profitability analysis.

Consider your business requirements and growth trajectory when choosing a plan. If you anticipate expanding your operations or needing advanced features in the future, it may be beneficial to opt for a higher-tier plan from the outset. Additionally, assess the number of users who will need access to QuickBooks Online, as each plan has limitations on user access.

It's important to review subscription plans regularly, especially during periods of business growth or change. QuickBooks may introduce new features or plans that better align with your evolving needs. Regularly reassessing your subscription ensures that you are getting the most value out of the platform and are equipped with the tools necessary for effective financial management.

Key Points:

    1. Consider factors such as business size, financial

complexity, and budget when choosing a QuickBooks Online subscription plan.

2. Evaluate available plans like Simple Start, Essentials, and Plus, each offering different features.

3. Anticipate future needs and growth to choose a plan that accommodates potential expansions in operations.

4. Regularly review subscription plans to align with changes in business requirements and take advantage of new features.

1.3.3 Customizing Your Company QuickBooks Online Settings

Customizing your company settings in QuickBooks Online is an essential step to tailor the platform to your specific business processes and preferences. QuickBooks provides a range of customization options, allowing users to configure settings related to invoicing, expenses, taxes, and more.

Start by navigating to the settings menu within QuickBooks Online. Here, you'll find various tabs, each corresponding to different aspects of your business settings. Begin with the "Company Settings" tab, where you can input details such as your business address, phone number, and other contact information. This ensures that your business details are accurately reflected on documents like invoices and reports.

Next, delve into the "Sales" settings to customize the way you invoice customers. QuickBooks allows you to choose invoice templates, set invoice numbering preferences, and specify default payment terms. These customizations not only enhance the professional appearance of your invoices but also streamline your billing process.

In the "Expenses" settings, configure options related to expense tracking, such as preferred expense accounts and categories. Ensure that tax-related settings are accurately configured to align with your business's tax obligations. This includes specifying your tax agency and setting up tax rates based on your location and applicable regulations.

As you explore the customization options, take advantage of features like automated email messages, which can be personalized to communicate effectively with customers. Additionally, explore integrations with other tools and apps that can enhance the functionality of QuickBooks Online, such as payment processors and project management tools.

Regularly revisit your company settings to accommodate changes in your business model or requirements. Adjusting settings ensures that QuickBooks Online continues to align with your evolving needs and provides an optimal experience for financial management.

Key Points:

1. Access the settings menu in QuickBooks Online to customize various aspects of your company's configuration.

2. Input accurate business information in the "Company Settings" tab to reflect on documents like invoices and reports.

3. Customize invoicing preferences, including

templates, invoice numbering, and payment terms, in the "Sales" settings.

4. Configure expense tracking options, tax-related settings, and personalized email messages in the relevant tabs.

5. Explore integrations with other tools and regularly revisit settings to accommodate changes in business requirements.

1.4 Navigating The Quickbooks Online Dashboard

1.4.1 Understanding the Dashboard Layout

Understanding the dashboard layout is fundamental for efficient navigation and utilization of any digital interface. Dashboards are designed to provide an at-a-glance view of essential information or metrics. Typically, they consist of multiple components such as widgets, cards, or panels, each displaying specific data sets or functionalities. The layout's effectiveness lies in its ability to organize information in a visually comprehensible manner.

The top portion of a dashboard often includes key performance indicators (KPIs) or summary information that gives an immediate snapshot of critical metrics. This section aims to offer a quick overview, enabling users to grasp the current status without delving deeper. It might contain charts, graphs, or numerical summaries showcasing data trends or essential figures.

Moving down the dashboard, you may encounter various modules or sections, each devoted to specific categories or functionalities. These sections might include data tables, visual representations like graphs or charts, embedded reports, or interactive elements facilitating user engagement.

The layout's customization is crucial to meet diverse user needs. Often, dashboards allow for personalization, enabling users to rearrange, resize, or remove components based on their preferences. This adaptability ensures that the most critical information is easily accessible, fostering efficiency in decision-making processes.

Understanding the hierarchy and placement of different elements within the dashboard layout enhances user experience and enables better interaction with the provided information. It empowers users to quickly locate and interpret the data they require, facilitating informed decision-making and improved productivity.

1.4.2 Key Navigation Features

Efficient navigation within a dashboard is vital to streamline the user experience and maximize productivity. Navigational features encompass various tools and functionalities that facilitate movement between different sections or elements of the dashboard.

Menus and sidebars often serve as primary navigation elements, offering access to different areas or modules within the dashboard. These menus may use collapsible sections or dropdown lists to organize content hierarchically, allowing users to navigate through various levels of information.

Hyperlinks or clickable elements within the dashboard enable users to quickly move from one section to another or access detailed information. These hyperlinks can lead to specific reports, drill-down pages, or external resources, enhancing the dashboard's functionality and versatility.

Search functionalities integrated into dashboards allow users to locate specific data or information swiftly. Search bars or filters help users narrow down vast datasets, enabling them to focus on the information they require without the need for manual exploration.

Another crucial navigation feature is breadcrumb trails, which show the user's path through the dashboard. This tool helps users understand their current location within the dashboard's structure and easily backtrack or navigate to higher-level sections.

Moreover, shortcuts or hotkeys can significantly boost navigation efficiency for power users. These shortcuts, when appropriately implemented, allow users to perform actions or switch between sections quickly, reducing reliance on mouse-based interactions.

The effective combination and implementation of these navigation features contribute to a seamless and user-friendly experience, ensuring that users can effortlessly move around the dashboard to access relevant information.

1.4.3 Personalizing Your Dashboard for Efficiency

Personalization plays a pivotal role in enhancing user experience by tailoring the dashboard to individual preferences and needs. Customization options empower users to configure the dashboard layout, content, and functionalities according to their specific requirements, leading to increased efficiency and usability.

Widgets or modules that offer flexibility in arrangement and size enable users to prioritize the display of crucial information. Being able to move, resize, or remove components allows users to create a personalized layout that aligns with their workflow and preferences.

Furthermore, customizable settings for data visualization, such as color schemes, chart types, or display formats, cater to individual preferences. Users can choose visualization options that resonate with their visual interpretation, making data analysis more intuitive and accessible.

The ability to create personalized dashboards or templates saves time by presenting users with relevant information immediately upon logging in. Custom dashboards can be designed for specific roles or tasks, ensuring that users have quick access to the most pertinent data for their responsibilities.

Moreover, user-specific preferences, such as language settings, default views, or personalized alerts and notifications, contribute to a more tailored and efficient dashboard experience. These personalized settings streamline workflow and reduce the time needed to locate critical information.

Ultimately, the value of personalization lies in its ability to enhance user satisfaction and productivity. By allowing users to shape their dashboard environment to suit their unique needs, personalization fosters a sense of ownership and control, leading to more effective utilization of the dashboard's capabilities.

GETTING STARTED WITH COMPANY SETUP

2.1 Creating Your Company Profile

C reating a company profile is a critical step for any business, as it serves as an introduction to potential clients, partners, and investors. It encapsulates essential information about your company, its values, mission, and what sets it apart from competitors. To begin, gather comprehensive details about your business, including its name, address, industry, founding date, mission statement, and a brief overview of products or services offered. It's important to ensure accuracy and consistency while inputting this information, as it forms the foundation of your company's identity.

The business description should be concise yet comprehensive, providing an overview of what your company does, its target market, unique selling proposition (USP), and future aspirations. This section is an opportunity to showcase your company's strengths, specialization, and competitive advantages. Presenting a clear and compelling narrative helps stakeholders understand the essence of your business and its positioning in the market.

Incorporating testimonials, client success stories, or notable achievements can add credibility to your company profile. Highlighting awards, recognitions, or certifications attained further solidifies your company's reputation and expertise in the industry. Additionally, including visuals such as high-quality images, infographics, or videos can enhance the profile, making it more engaging and visually appealing.

2.1.1 Inputting Business Information

Inputting accurate and detailed business information forms the backbone of your company profile. It encompasses fundamental details like the legal name of the business, registration number, physical address, and operational locations. Ensure that the information aligns with official documents to avoid discrepancies that might lead to confusion or distrust among stakeholders.

Providing an insightful overview of your business's history, evolution, and milestones achieved can add depth to the profile. Mentioning the founding story, major milestones, expansions, or significant changes in the business trajectory humanizes the brand, fostering connections with the audience. Detailing the company's organizational structure, leadership team, and key personnel establishes transparency and showcases the expertise driving the company's success.

When inputting financial information, exercise caution and share only what is necessary. Highlighting revenue figures, growth rates, or financial projections can be crucial for potential investors or partners but should be disclosed prudently to maintain confidentiality and competitive advantage.

2.1.2 Uploading Your Company Logo

The company logo is a visual representation of your brand and plays a pivotal role in brand recognition and recall. When uploading your company logo, ensure it adheres to quality standards and effectively reflects your brand's identity. The logo should be unique, memorable, and scalable to maintain its integrity across various mediums and sizes.

Consider the color palette, typography, and symbolism incorporated in the logo to ensure it aligns with your brand's values, ethos, and target audience. A well-designed logo communicates professionalism, credibility, and creates a lasting impression. It should be versatile enough to be displayed on different platforms, from digital media to print materials, without compromising its visual appeal or message.

2.1.3 Setting Up Contact Details

Setting up accurate and accessible contact details is crucial for establishing communication channels with potential clients, partners, or investors. Include multiple modes of contact such as phone numbers, email addresses, physical addresses, and links to social media profiles or websites. Ensure these details are regularly updated to prevent missed opportunities or frustration among stakeholders trying to reach out.

Consider creating specific contact points for different purposes, such as sales inquiries, customer support, or partnership proposals, to streamline communication and ensure queries are directed to the relevant departments or individuals. Implementing a user-friendly contact form on your website can simplify the process for visitors to reach out, providing a convenient and efficient way to engage with your company.

Offering clear instructions or a map for physical locations, along with operating hours, demonstrates transparency and accessibility. Additionally, incorporating a responsive customer service approach, promptly addressing inquiries or feedback, fosters positive relationships and reflects a customer-centric ethos.

2.2 Defining Your Chart of Accounts

The chart of accounts is a structured listing of all financial accounts used by a business, categorizing transactions to facilitate financial reporting and analysis. It serves as the backbone of the accounting system, organizing accounts into assets, liabilities, equity, revenues, and expenses. Defining a comprehensive chart of accounts tailored to your business's specific needs is vital for accurate financial recording and reporting.

The chart of accounts typically includes a numerical or alphanumeric code assigned to each account for easy identification and reference. Segregating accounts based on their nature and function enables better tracking, analysis, and interpretation of financial data. This segregation might encompass categories such as cash, accounts receivable, inventory, operating expenses, and more detailed subcategories within these main accounts.

Furthermore, establishing clear accounting policies and procedures ensures consistency and standardization in financial record-keeping. This involves defining guidelines for recording transactions, handling accounts, and maintaining compliance with regulatory standards. Regular reviews and updates of the chart of accounts are essential to accommodate changes in business operations, expansion, or evolving accounting practices.

Implementing a robust chart of accounts facilitates efficient financial management, budgeting, and decision-making. It enables the generation of accurate financial statements, including balance sheets, income statements, and cash flow statements, providing invaluable insights for strategic planning and informed business decisions.

2.2.1 Understanding Chart of Accounts Basics

The Chart of Accounts (COA) is a fundamental element in accounting that organizes a company's financial transactions. It serves as a comprehensive listing of all accounts used by a business to record financial transactions in its accounting system. Typically, the COA includes assets, liabilities, equity, revenue, and expense accounts. Each account is assigned a unique code or number for easy identification and tracking.

Components of a Chart of Accounts

1. **Assets**: These are resources owned by the company, such as cash, inventory, property, and equipment. They are typically listed first in the COA.

2. **Liabilities**: Debts or obligations owed by the company, including loans, accounts payable, and

accrued expenses.

3. **Equity**: Represents the net value of the company and includes items like owner's equity or retained earnings.

4. **Revenue**: Income generated by the company from its primary business activities.

5. **Expenses**: Costs incurred to generate revenue, including salaries, utilities, and supplies.

Importance of a Well-Structured COA

A well-organized Chart of Accounts is crucial for accurate financial reporting, tax compliance, and strategic decision-making. It allows businesses to categorize and track financial transactions efficiently, providing a clear overview of the company's financial health. Properly structured accounts enable easier analysis and comparison of financial data, facilitating informed business decisions.

Understanding the COA basics ensures that financial data is recorded accurately and consistently, enhancing the reliability of financial statements and enabling stakeholders to assess the company's performance and make informed decisions.

2.2.2 Adding and Customizing Accounts

Adding and customizing accounts within the Chart of Accounts is a crucial aspect of tailoring the accounting system to suit a company's specific needs. Most accounting software allows for the addition and customization of accounts to align with the unique financial structure and reporting requirements of the business.

Steps for Adding Accounts:

1. **Identification of Needs**: Evaluate the specific financial information that requires tracking. Determine if new accounts are necessary for proper categorization.

2. **Choosing Account Type**: Select the appropriate account type (e.g., asset, liability, revenue, expense) based on the nature of the transactions to be recorded.

3. **Assigning Account Codes**: Allocate unique codes or numbers to the new accounts for easy identification and organization within the COA.

Customization of Accounts:

Businesses often customize accounts to align with their operational nuances. This customization may involve:

- **Subdividing Accounts**: Breaking down broader categories into more detailed subcategories. For instance, under expenses, separate accounts for utilities, rent, and office supplies could be created for more precise tracking.

- **Naming Conventions**: Using specific and descriptive names for accounts to ensure clarity and easy identification of transactions.

- **Hierarchy Structure**: Establishing a hierarchical structure within the COA, with parent and subaccounts, to organize accounts in a logical and systematic manner.

2.2.3 Organizing Accounts for Clarity

Organizing accounts within the Chart of Accounts is essential for maintaining clarity, accuracy, and ease of use in financial reporting and analysis. Effective organization allows for efficient data entry, retrieval, and analysis, streamlining the accounting processes.

Strategies for Organizing Accounts:

1. **Logical Grouping**: Group similar accounts together, such as all asset accounts or all revenue accounts, to simplify financial analysis and reporting.

2. **Consistent Naming Conventions**: Use consistent and standardized naming conventions for accounts throughout the COA to avoid confusion and ensure uniformity.

3. **Numeric or Alphanumeric Order**: Arrange accounts numerically or alphabetically for ease of reference. This method aids in locating specific accounts quickly.

4. **Hierarchical Structure**: Establish a hierarchical structure with parent and child accounts. This arrangement facilitates a clear understanding of the relationship between different accounts.

5. **Regular Review and Adjustment**: Periodically review and adjust the COA to accommodate changes in the business structure, ensuring relevance and accuracy.

2.3 Configuring Sales Settings

Configuring sales settings within an accounting system is vital to accurately record and track revenue generated from sales transactions. These settings allow businesses to customize how sales are processed, documented, and reported in the accounting software.

Key Components of Sales Settings Configuration:

1. **Sales Tax Settings**: Configure tax rates, exemptions, and rules applicable to sales

transactions based on the company's location and tax regulations.

2. **Payment Terms and Methods**: Define payment terms (e.g., net 30 days, immediate payment) and accepted payment methods (cash, credit card, checks) for sales transactions.

3. **Sales Categories or Products**: Categorize sales transactions based on products, services, or departments. This categorization aids in analyzing sales performance.

4. **Invoicing Settings**: Customize invoice templates, numbering sequences, and layouts for professional and standardized invoicing.

5. **Integration with Sales Platforms**: Integrate the accounting system with sales platforms or POS systems for seamless data transfer and accurate recording of sales transactions.

Configuring sales settings accurately ensures that revenue from sales is recorded correctly, taxes are applied appropriately, and financial reports provide an accurate representation of the company's sales performance. It streamlines the sales process and facilitates efficient financial management.

2.3.1 Setting Up Products and Services

Setting up products and services is a fundamental aspect of any business, whether it's a physical store or an online platform. It involves meticulously listing and organizing the items or services offered by the business. The process typically starts with creating a catalog that includes detailed information about each product or service. This includes product names, descriptions, prices, images, SKUs (Stock Keeping Units), and other relevant attributes.

One crucial aspect of setting up products and services is categorization. Products can be grouped into categories and subcategories, making it easier for customers to navigate through the offerings. This organization enhances the user experience, allowing customers to find what they need more efficiently.

Moreover, setting up products and services often involves determining inventory levels and managing stock. Businesses need to monitor their inventory to ensure they don't oversell products and disappoint customers. Utilizing inventory management systems or software can streamline this process, providing real-time updates on stock levels and facilitating reordering when necessary.

Additionally, businesses might consider incorporating variations of products, such as different sizes, colors, or configurations. These variations can be managed within the product setup, enabling customers to choose the specific options that suit their preferences.

2.3.2 Creating Price Lists and Discounts

Creating price lists and offering discounts are critical strategies in marketing and sales. Businesses need to set competitive and profitable prices for their products or services. Developing pricing strategies involves considering various factors like production costs, market demand, competitor prices, and perceived value.

Price lists are structured catalogs that display the prices of different items or services. They often categorize products and services along with their respective prices, making it easier for customers to compare and choose.

Some businesses might implement dynamic pricing, where prices change based on market conditions, demand, or other factors.

Discounts play a significant role in attracting customers and boosting sales. Businesses can offer discounts in various forms such as percentage-based discounts, buy-one-get-one (BOGO) offers, seasonal promotions, or loyalty rewards. These incentives not only attract new customers but also retain existing ones.

It's crucial to strategize discounts effectively, ensuring they don't negatively impact profitability. Discounts should be balanced to stimulate sales without significantly reducing profit margins. Moreover, businesses should communicate discounts clearly to customers through various channels like websites, emails, or advertisements.

2.3.3 Integrating Payment Gateways

Integrating payment gateways is essential for businesses operating online, enabling secure and efficient transactions. Payment gateways are platforms or services that facilitate the authorization of payment between the customer and the business. They encrypt sensitive financial information, ensuring secure transmission during online transactions.

Selecting the right payment gateway involves considering factors like transaction fees, security features, supported currencies, ease of use, and compatibility with the business's website or platform. Popular payment gateways include PayPal, Stripe, Square, and others, each offering different features and functionalities.

Integration of payment gateways requires technical expertise or the assistance of developers. Businesses need to ensure seamless integration to provide customers with a smooth checkout experience. Testing the payment process is crucial to identify and resolve any issues before going live.

Additionally, offering multiple payment options can cater to a wider customer base. Accepting credit/ debit cards, digital wallets, bank transfers, and other methods enhances convenience for customers, potentially increasing conversion rates.

2.4 Managing Users and Permissions

Managing users and permissions involves controlling access to various functionalities and data within a system or platform. Businesses often have different user roles such as administrators, managers, employees, and customers, each requiring specific permissions based on their responsibilities and needs.

Implementing robust user management systems allows administrators to create, modify, or delete user accounts, assign roles, and regulate access levels. Permissions can be categorized into read, write, edit, or delete, depending on the user's role and requirements.

Moreover, businesses may need to integrate Single Sign-On (SSO) solutions for streamlined user access across multiple platforms or applications. SSO enables users to log in once and access various interconnected systems without the need for multiple credentials.

Security is paramount in user management. Implementing measures like multi-factor authentication, regular access reviews, and encryption of sensitive data ensures protection against unauthorized access and potential breaches.

Auditing user activities and maintaining logs can provide insights into user behavior and potential security risks. Regularly reviewing and updating user permissions based on changes in roles or responsibilities within the organization is crucial for maintaining data security and integrity.

Each of these aspects - setting up products and services, creating price lists and discounts, integrating payment gateways, and managing users and permissions - forms integral parts of managing and operating a successful business, whether it's in a physical or digital landscape. Mastering these components allows businesses to streamline operations, enhance customer satisfaction, and drive growth in a competitive market

2.4.1 Adding Team Members

The process of adding team members to a project or organization involves more than just integrating individuals. It's about weaving a collective tapestry of skills, experiences, and perspectives that contribute to the synergy of a team. Adding new members can invigorate a team with fresh ideas, skills, and energy. It's a delicate balance of fitting the right person into the puzzle while ensuring cohesion and collaboration within the existing team dynamics.

When incorporating new members, it's pivotal to consider several aspects:

1. **Skills and Expertise**: Assess the skills required for the project or team. It's essential to match the abilities of new members with the existing gaps in the team. Whether it's technical expertise,

creative thinking, or leadership skills, aligning these with the team's goals is crucial.

2. **Cultural Fit**: Beyond technical capabilities, ensuring a cultural fit is equally important. A cohesive team works well when its members share common values, work ethics, and communication styles. Integrating someone who aligns with these aspects can foster a sense of belonging and enhance team cohesion.

3. **Onboarding Process**: Facilitating a smooth onboarding process is vital. It includes introducing new team members to existing workflows, tools, and methodologies. This phase not only eases their transition but also allows them to understand their role and contributions effectively.

4. **Communication and Collaboration**: Establishing clear lines of communication and encouraging collaboration is imperative. Whether it's through team meetings, digital collaboration platforms, or regular check-ins, creating an environment where team members feel comfortable sharing ideas and feedback fosters a more productive and innovative atmosphere.

5. **Feedback and Adaptation**: Continuously seeking feedback from both new and existing team members is key to adaptation and improvement. Encouraging an open dialogue allows for adjustments, ensuring that everyone feels valued and heard within the team.

Adding team members isn't merely about filling positions; it's about enriching the collective capabilities and enhancing the team's overall performance.

2.4.2 Assigning User Roles and Permissions

Assigning user roles and permissions is the cornerstone of data security and effective management within any system or platform. It delineates the level of access and authority individuals have within an organization's digital infrastructure. Striking a balance between granting adequate access for efficient workflow and safeguarding sensitive information is crucial.

Several points need consideration while assigning roles and permissions:

1. **Role-Based Access Control (RBAC)**: RBAC is a methodology that defines access permissions to system resources based on job roles. Each role has its set of permissions, ensuring that individuals can access only the necessary information to perform their duties. This minimizes the risk of unauthorized access to critical data.

2. **Least Privilege Principle**: Adhering to the principle of least privilege means granting the minimum level of access necessary for individuals to perform their tasks. This minimizes the potential impact of a security breach by restricting unnecessary access.

3. **Regular Auditing and Updates**: Regularly auditing user roles and permissions is vital. As roles within an organization evolve, so do access requirements. Conducting periodic reviews and

updates ensures that access remains aligned with current responsibilities and organizational changes.

4. **Training and Awareness**: Educating users about the importance of adhering to their designated roles and permissions is crucial. Training sessions on data security practices and the consequences of improper access can significantly reduce accidental breaches.

5. **Emergency Access Protocols**: Establishing protocols for emergency access is necessary in case of unforeseen situations or urgent requirements. However, this should be tightly controlled and monitored to prevent misuse.

Balancing accessibility and security is an ongoing challenge in assigning user roles and permissions, demanding continual evaluation and fine-tuning of access levels.

2.4.3 Ensuring Data Security and Privacy

Data security and privacy are paramount concerns in today's interconnected digital landscape. With the increasing volume of data generated and stored, ensuring its security and privacy is a multifaceted endeavor involving technological, procedural, and compliance measures.

Here are essential aspects to consider for ensuring data security and privacy:

1. **Encryption and Authentication**: Implementing robust encryption methods and multi-factor authentication fortifies data security. Encrypting sensitive information both in transit and at rest

minimizes the risk of unauthorized access or data breaches.

2. **Data Governance Policies**: Establishing comprehensive data governance policies outlines how data is collected, processed, stored, and shared. These policies ensure compliance with regulations and define roles and responsibilities for data management.

3. **Regular Security Assessments and Audits**: Conducting regular security assessments and audits helps identify vulnerabilities and weaknesses in systems and processes. It allows for proactive measures to strengthen security measures and address potential risks before they are exploited.

4. **Compliance with Regulations**: Adhering to data protection regulations and standards, such as GDPR, HIPAA, or CCPA, is non-negotiable. Compliance ensures that data is handled ethically, transparently, and in accordance with legal requirements.

5. **Employee Training and Awareness**: Educating employees about data security best practices is pivotal. Human error remains a significant cause of data breaches, making ongoing training and awareness campaigns essential in mitigating risks.

6. **Incident Response and Recovery Plans**: Despite preventive measures, incidents may occur. Having robust response and recovery plans in place helps minimize the impact of data breaches, enabling swift action to mitigate damages and

restore systems.

Safeguarding data security and privacy demands a holistic approach, combining technological advancements, procedural measures, compliance adherence, and a vigilant mindset to combat evolving threats

RECORDING FINANCIAL TRANSACTIONS

3.1 Entering Sales and Invoices

Sales and invoices are pivotal components of any business transaction, representing the exchange of goods or services for monetary value. The process of creating invoices and recording sales receipts forms the core of financial documentation within a company.

3.1.1 Creating Invoices for Goods and Services

The creation of invoices involves a systematic approach to detail the goods or services provided, their quantity, price, terms of payment, and essential business information. Accuracy and clarity are paramount to avoid discrepancies or misunderstandings between parties involved. To create an effective invoice, it's crucial to include:

- **Identification Details**: The invoice should bear unique identifiers like an invoice number, date of issuance, and relevant contact information for both the seller and the buyer.
- **Itemized Goods/Services**: A detailed breakdown of the goods or services rendered, including their descriptions, quantities, rates, and subtotal for

each line item.

- **Terms and Conditions**: Explicitly state the payment terms, including due dates, acceptable payment methods, any discounts or penalties for early or late payments, and additional terms of sale.
- **Total Amount Due**: Sum up all the costs, including taxes and any applicable fees, to provide a clear total amount owed.

Creating professional and comprehensive invoices not only ensures prompt payment but also serves as a legal record of the transaction, benefiting both parties in case of any disputes or discrepancies.

3.1.2 Recording Sales Receipts

Recording sales receipts accurately is imperative for maintaining financial transparency and tracking revenue. Sales receipts provide a detailed record of each transaction completed by the business. Key elements to include when recording sales receipts are:

- **Transaction Details**: Date of the sale, the mode of payment, and a breakdown of the items or services sold.
- **Customer Information**: The name or identification of the buyer, their contact details, and any pertinent customer account numbers or references.
- **Payment Confirmation**: Acknowledgment of the payment received, specifying the amount and the payment method utilized.
- **Salesperson/Employee Details**: If applicable, note the employee responsible for the sale to track performance and commissions accurately.

Efficient recording of sales receipts facilitates the reconciliation of accounts, helps in analyzing sales patterns, and ensures that all income generated is properly accounted for in the financial records of the business.

3.1.3 Handling Refunds and Returns

Refunds and returns are inherent parts of any sales process, necessitating a structured approach to ensure customer satisfaction while maintaining financial integrity. Handling refunds and returns involves several steps:

- **Clear Policies**: Establish transparent policies regarding refunds and returns to manage customer expectations. Clearly communicate these policies on receipts, invoices, or the company's website.

- **Documentation**: Maintain detailed records of returned items, reasons for return, and refund transactions. This documentation is crucial for accounting purposes and analyzing trends in returns.

- **Timely Processing**: Process refunds promptly upon receiving returned goods or acknowledging the return request. This fosters trust and goodwill with customers.

- **Quality Control and Improvement**: Analyze patterns in returns to identify potential issues with products or services. Use this data to improve quality and customer satisfaction.

Effective handling of refunds and returns is vital for customer retention and satisfaction. It also contributes to maintaining a positive brand image and aids in refining business practices for continuous improvement.

3.2 Managing Expenses and Bills

Managing expenses and bills is an essential aspect of financial management for any business. Efficient handling of expenses involves tracking, organizing, and optimizing the various costs incurred in operating a business.

Proper management of expenses and bills involves several key strategies:

- **Budgeting and Forecasting**: Develop a comprehensive budget that outlines expected expenses across different categories. Regularly review and adjust these budgets based on actual expenditures and revenue forecasts.

- **Expense Tracking**: Implement robust systems or software to accurately track all business expenses. Categorize expenses to gain insights into where the money is being spent, enabling informed decision-making.

- **Timely Payment of Bills**: Ensure that bills are paid on time to avoid late fees or disruptions in services. Implementing automated payment systems can streamline this process and prevent oversights.

- **Expense Reduction Strategies**: Continuously assess expenses to identify areas where costs can be reduced or optimized without compromising quality or operational efficiency.

By effectively managing expenses and bills, businesses can maintain financial stability, improve cash flow management, and make informed strategic decisions for sustainable growth and profitability

3.2.1 Entering Bills and Supplier Invoices

Entering bills and supplier invoices is a critical aspect of managing finances within any business, ensuring accurate tracking and timely payment of obligations. In QuickBooks Online, this process involves capturing incoming invoices from suppliers, encompassing details such as the invoice number, date, due date, amount owed, and relevant item descriptions or services rendered.

When initiating this process, QuickBooks Online users can navigate to the "Expenses" tab and select "Vendors." Here, they can choose "Enter Bill" or "Supplier Invoice," depending on the specific terminology used by the platform. The user then fills in the required fields, ensuring precision in data entry to avoid discrepancies in accounting records. This meticulousness is crucial for maintaining the integrity of financial reports and ensuring compliance with payable deadlines.

It's pivotal to cross-verify the accuracy of information inputted against the received invoices to prevent errors or discrepancies that might lead to incorrect payment or accounting inaccuracies. QuickBooks Online streamlines this by allowing users to attach the actual invoice document for future reference, ensuring a comprehensive audit trail.

One of the key advantages of using QuickBooks Online for bill entry is the ability to track and manage bills in one centralized location. This centralization minimizes the risk of overlooking payments or duplicate entries, providing a clear overview of outstanding liabilities, aiding in better cash flow management, and facilitating timely payments to vendors.

3.2.2 Tracking Expenses and Receipts

Tracking expenses and receipts within QuickBooks Online is an essential aspect of maintaining accurate financial records and gaining insights into business spending patterns. The platform offers multiple avenues for expense tracking, accommodating various payment methods such as credit cards, bank transfers, and cash transactions.

Users can leverage the "Banking" tab within QuickBooks Online to directly connect bank accounts and credit cards, enabling automatic importing and categorization of transactions. This feature expedites the tracking process, reducing manual entry and ensuring real-time visibility into expenses.

Moreover, QuickBooks Online allows users to capture and digitize paper receipts efficiently. Through the mobile app or by directly uploading scanned receipts, users can associate expenses with relevant transactions, categorize them by type (e.g., office supplies, travel expenses, utilities), and allocate them to specific projects or clients.

Categorization and proper labeling of expenses play a pivotal role in financial reporting and analysis. QuickBooks Online allows for the creation of custom expense categories, tailoring the platform to suit the unique needs of different businesses. This customization assists in generating detailed reports that provide insights into spending patterns, aiding in budgeting, forecasting, and identifying areas for cost optimization.

3.2.3 Utilizing Purchase Orders

Utilizing purchase orders (POs) in QuickBooks Online is instrumental in managing procurement processes and fostering transparent communication between buyers and suppliers. POs serve as legally binding documents outlining specific goods or services to be purchased, including quantities, prices, delivery dates, and terms of the agreement.

Within QuickBooks Online, creating purchase orders involves accessing the "Expenses" tab, selecting "Vendors," and choosing the "Create Purchase Order" option. Users input essential details, such as vendor information, item descriptions, quantities, and agreed-upon prices. This systematic approach ensures clarity and alignment between the buyer and supplier, reducing the chances of misunderstandings or disputes.

The utilization of POs in QuickBooks Online offers several benefits, including enhanced inventory management and control. By associating purchase orders with inventory items, businesses can track stock levels, monitor pending orders, and optimize inventory replenishment, ensuring adequate stock availability without overstocking.

Furthermore, POs facilitate better budgetary control and expense forecasting. By formalizing procurement processes through POs, businesses gain visibility into committed expenses, aiding in cash flow planning and financial decision-making. Additionally, POs serve as crucial documentation for auditing purposes, ensuring compliance and accountability in purchasing activities.

3.3 Bank Reconciliation in QuickBooks Online

Bank reconciliation in QuickBooks Online is a fundamental process that ensures the accuracy and consistency between a company's financial records and bank statements.

This process involves matching transactions recorded in QuickBooks with the corresponding entries in bank statements to identify discrepancies and reconcile any differences.

QuickBooks Online simplifies bank reconciliation by offering a user-friendly interface where users can link their bank accounts and credit cards. Once connected, the platform automatically imports transactions, allowing for easy comparison and reconciliation against the records in QuickBooks.

The reconciliation process involves reviewing each transaction to confirm whether it matches the corresponding entry in the bank statement. Any discrepancies, such as missing transactions, duplicate entries, or errors in amounts, need to be meticulously investigated and rectified to ensure accurate financial reporting.

One of the crucial benefits of bank reconciliation in QuickBooks Online is its ability to identify and rectify discrepancies promptly. This process aids in uncovering potential errors, fraudulent activities, or bank fees that might have been overlooked, ensuring the financial integrity of the business.

Furthermore, regular and timely bank reconciliation using QuickBooks Online provides businesses with a clear understanding of their cash flow status. It aids in identifying outstanding payments, deposits, and other financial activities, enabling informed decision-making and fostering financial stability.

3.3.1 Connecting Bank and Credit Card Accounts

Connecting bank and credit card accounts in financial software like QuickBooks Online is crucial for accurate bookkeeping. This process involves linking your accounts to the software, enabling automatic importing of transactions, which aids in tracking expenses, income, and maintaining financial records efficiently.

By linking your bank and credit card accounts, you streamline the data entry process, reducing human error and ensuring that all transactions are recorded promptly. It allows for real-time monitoring of cash flow, which is essential for making informed financial decisions. Moreover, the connection facilitates reconciling transactions with bank statements, providing a clear overview of your financial standing.

The process of connecting accounts often involves providing login credentials or using secure methods of authentication to establish a direct connection between your financial institution and QuickBooks Online. This connectivity is encrypted and secure, ensuring the confidentiality and integrity of sensitive financial information.

3.3.2 Reconciling Transactions with Bank Statements

Reconciling transactions with bank statements is an essential part of financial management, ensuring accuracy and completeness in your records. This process involves comparing the transactions recorded in QuickBooks Online with the entries on your bank statements, aiming to identify any discrepancies or errors.

To reconcile transactions effectively, start by reviewing the beginning and ending balances in QuickBooks Online against the corresponding figures in your bank statements.

Then, meticulously match each transaction, ensuring that deposits, withdrawals, and other transactions align accurately.

Discrepancies may arise due to various reasons, such as timing differences in transaction processing between your financial institution and QuickBooks Online, bank fees, outstanding checks, or data entry errors. It's crucial to investigate any discrepancies promptly to rectify them and maintain accurate financial records.

Reconciling transactions not only helps in identifying errors but also enhances the credibility of financial reports, making them reliable for decision-making and analysis.

3.3.3 Resolving Discrepancies and Errors

Resolving discrepancies and errors in financial records is imperative to ensure the accuracy and integrity of your data. When discrepancies arise between your QuickBooks Online records and bank statements, a systematic approach is essential to pinpoint and rectify the issues.

Firstly, carefully review the transactions in question, comparing the details in QuickBooks Online with the corresponding entries in your bank statements. Pay close attention to transaction dates, amounts, and descriptions to identify any discrepancies accurately.

If the discrepancy is due to a timing difference or a processing delay between the software and your bank, consider reconciling the transactions over a different time frame or reaching out to your bank for clarification.

For errors stemming from data entry mistakes or misclassification of transactions, make the necessary adjustments in QuickBooks Online. It's crucial to maintain clear documentation of any modifications made to ensure a transparent audit trail and accurate financial reporting.

Regularly reconciling accounts and promptly addressing discrepancies not only maintains the accuracy of financial records but also fosters better financial management and decision-making.

3.4 Handling Payroll and Employee Payments

Handling payroll and employee payments is a critical aspect of business operations that necessitates accuracy, compliance, and efficiency. QuickBooks Online provides tools to streamline this process, covering aspects from setting up payroll to managing taxes and deductions.

3.4.1 Setting Up Payroll in QuickBooks Online

Setting up payroll in QuickBooks Online involves several steps to ensure accurate and compliant payroll processing. Begin by entering essential company information, including tax identification numbers, employee details, and payroll schedules.

Next, configure payroll settings such as pay frequency, payment methods, and employee deductions. Accurately inputting wage information, overtime rates, and any additional earnings or benefits ensures precise calculation of employee pay.

Additionally, QuickBooks Online assists in setting up direct deposit for employees, enabling seamless and secure payment transactions. Verify and review all details thoroughly to avoid errors in payroll processing.

3.4.2 Processing Employee Payments

Processing employee payments through QuickBooks Online streamlines the payroll process, offering various payment methods while ensuring accuracy and compliance. Once payroll details are entered and verified, the software calculates employee wages, taxes, and deductions automatically.

The system generates pay stubs and direct deposit payments, providing employees with clear documentation of their earnings and deductions. This simplifies the payment process and enhances transparency between employers and employees.

QuickBooks Online also enables the issuance of physical checks if required, giving businesses flexibility in their payment methods. Regularly reviewing and confirming the accuracy of payments before finalizing them is crucial to avoid discrepancies or errors in employee compensation.

3.4.3 Managing Payroll Taxes and Deductions

Managing payroll taxes and deductions is a complex yet essential aspect of payroll processing. QuickBooks Online assists in accurately calculating and withholding federal, state, and local taxes based on employee information and the company's location.

The software also aids in managing deductions such as healthcare premiums, retirement contributions, and other voluntary withholdings. Ensuring compliance with tax regulations and staying updated with tax law changes is vital to avoid penalties or errors in tax filings.

QuickBooks Online generates tax forms, such as W-2s and 1099s, simplifying the reporting process at the end of the year. Regularly reviewing tax liabilities, filings, and ensuring timely payments to tax authorities are crucial to maintaining compliance and avoiding potential issues

UTILIZING REPORTING AND ANALYTICS

4.1 Generating Financial Reports

F inancial reporting is a fundamental aspect of any business's operations, crucial for understanding its financial health and performance. Among the core components of financial reporting are Balance Sheets and Income Statements and Cash Flow Statements, which provide distinct perspectives on a company's financial status.

4.1.1 Balance Sheets and Income Statements

Balance sheets and income statements serve as key documents in assessing a company's financial standing. A **balance sheet** presents a snapshot of a company's assets, liabilities, and shareholder equity at a specific point in time. It showcases the company's resources and obligations, delineating what it owns versus what it owes. Meanwhile, an **income statement** outlines revenues, expenses, gains, and losses over a defined period, typically a quarter or a year, enabling stakeholders to evaluate the profitability of the business.

Balance sheets are structured with assets listed on one side (including cash, inventory, property) and liabilities on the other (like debts, accounts payable). The equation 'Assets = Liabilities + Equity' underscores the fundamental principle that the company's assets are financed by either debt or equity.

On the other hand, income statements depict the company's financial performance by detailing revenues earned and expenses incurred during a specific period. Revenue sources, such as sales, interest income, or service revenue, are showcased alongside expenses like operational costs, taxes, and interest payments. The net income, derived by subtracting expenses from revenues, signifies the profitability or loss incurred during that period.

Understanding these reports aids in decision-making, enabling management to pinpoint areas for improvement, assess financial stability, and plan for future growth.

4.1.2 Cash Flow Statements

While balance sheets and income statements are crucial, **cash flow statements** offer a distinct view of a company's financial health by tracking the movement of cash in and out of the business. This statement highlights the sources and uses of cash, categorized into operating, investing, and financing activities.

Operating activities encompass cash flows from core business operations, like revenue generation and operating expenses. Investing activities involve cash flows from the purchase or sale of assets, such as equipment or investments. Financing activities include cash flows related to debt, equity, and dividend payments.

The cash flow statement reveals how effectively a company manages its cash position, assesses its ability to cover obligations, and indicates whether it generates enough cash to sustain and expand operations. Analyzing cash flow patterns aids in evaluating liquidity, identifying potential cash flow issues, and strategizing for efficient cash management.

4.1.3 Customizing Reports for Your Business Needs

Tailoring financial reports to meet specific business needs is paramount. Different businesses might require customizations to focus on particular metrics, segments, or performance indicators relevant to their operations. Tools like accounting software offer options to personalize reports, allowing for the inclusion or exclusion of certain data, modification of formats, or creation of specialized reports for internal or external stakeholders.

Customized reports empower decision-makers by providing targeted insights that align with the company's goals and strategies. Whether it's analyzing sales performance, tracking project profitability, or assessing departmental expenses, customizable reports offer a personalized lens through which to evaluate and strategize for business success.

4.2 Analyzing Key Performance Indicators (KPIs)

Amidst the complexities of financial reporting, **Key Performance Indicators (KPIs)** stand as vital metrics used to measure and evaluate specific aspects of a business's performance.

4.2.1 Identifying Business Metrics

Identifying the right KPIs is crucial for effective decision-making and performance evaluation. KPIs vary across industries and businesses; they can range from financial metrics like revenue growth, profit margins, and return on investment (ROI), to operational metrics such as customer retention rates, inventory turnover, or employee productivity.

Each KPI serves as a compass guiding business actions, enabling managers to focus on areas that significantly impact performance. Identifying relevant KPIs involves aligning them with business objectives, ensuring they are measurable, achievable, and directly related to the company's success factors.

4.2.2 Utilizing QuickBooks Online Dashboards

QuickBooks Online provides intuitive dashboards that facilitate KPI tracking and analysis. These dashboards compile key financial data and metrics into visual representations, offering a real-time snapshot of the company's performance. Users can customize these dashboards to display preferred KPIs, graphs, and charts, providing a comprehensive overview or drilling down into specific metrics for detailed analysis.

The visual representation of KPIs through QuickBooks Online Dashboards simplifies the interpretation of complex financial data, empowering users to make informed decisions promptly. Moreover, it enables stakeholders to track trends, identify anomalies, and take proactive measures to steer the business in the desired direction.

4.2.3 Interpreting KPIs for Business Growth

Interpreting KPIs goes beyond merely tracking numbers; it involves understanding the story behind the data and leveraging insights to foster business growth. Analyzing KPI trends over time, comparing them against industry benchmarks, and conducting scenario analyses aid in identifying strengths, weaknesses, opportunities, and threats.

For instance, a declining sales growth KPI might prompt a review of marketing strategies or product offerings. Similarly, a high customer churn rate KPI might necessitate a deeper understanding of customer satisfaction and retention strategies. Effective interpretation of KPIs drives strategic decision-making, leading to improved operational efficiency, enhanced competitiveness, and sustained growth.

4.3 Budgeting and Forecasting

Budgeting and **forecasting** are integral components of financial management, enabling businesses to plan, allocate resources, and project future financial scenarios.

4.3.1 Creating and Managing Budgets

Creating a budget involves outlining expected revenues and allocating resources to various expenses and investments. It serves as a financial roadmap, guiding the allocation of funds to different departments or projects within a specified timeframe. Budgets can be created annually, quarterly, or monthly, allowing for detailed planning and control over expenditures.

A well-structured budget considers historical data, market trends, and business goals. It should be flexible enough to accommodate unforeseen changes while maintaining a balance between realistic goals and ambitious targets.

Managing budgets involves continuous monitoring, comparing actual expenditures against planned budgets, and making necessary adjustments to align with financial goals. This process helps in identifying variances, understanding their causes, and taking corrective actions to ensure financial objectives are met.

4.3.2 Comparing Actuals vs. Budgets

Analyzing the variance between actual financial outcomes and the budgeted figures provides valuable insights into a company's performance. Positive variances (where actuals exceed budgeted amounts) might indicate operational efficiency or unexpected revenue streams, while negative variances might signal overspending or revenue shortfalls.

Understanding these differences enables management to delve deeper into the underlying reasons and make informed decisions. It allows for adjustments to be made in strategies, resource allocation, or operational processes to ensure alignment with financial objectives and targets.

4.3.3 Forecasting Future Financial Scenarios

Forecasting involves predicting future financial outcomes based on historical data, current trends, and market analysis. It helps businesses anticipate potential challenges, opportunities, and trends that might impact financial performance.

There are various forecasting methods, from simple trend analysis to complex statistical models, each catering to different business needs. Accurate forecasting aids in proactive decision-making, enabling businesses to prepare for changing market conditions, manage risks effectively, and capitalize on emerging opportunities.

Businesses can utilize forecasts for resource allocation, setting realistic financial goals, and formulating strategic plans. By integrating forecasting into their financial planning process, companies enhance their ability to adapt and thrive in dynamic market environments.

4.4 Tax Preparation and Compliance

Tax preparation and **compliance** are critical aspects of financial management, ensuring businesses adhere to regulatory requirements while optimizing tax-related strategies.

4.4.1 Understanding Tax Categories and Codes

Understanding different tax categories and codes is essential for accurate tax reporting and compliance. Taxes can encompass income tax, sales tax, payroll tax, and more, each with its set of rules, regulations, and filing requirements.

Businesses need to stay abreast of changes in tax

laws and regulations to ensure compliance and avoid penalties. Utilizing accounting software or consulting tax professionals can aid in understanding the nuances of tax codes and categories relevant to the business.

4.4.2 Generating Tax Reports

Generating comprehensive tax reports is crucial for accurately reporting financial information to tax authorities. These reports compile relevant financial data in a format compliant with tax regulations, facilitating the preparation and filing of tax returns.

Accounting software often streamlines the process of generating tax reports by automatically categorizing transactions, calculating tax liabilities, and generating required forms and documents. This minimizes errors and ensures accurate tax reporting, thereby mitigating the risk of non-compliance.

4.4.3 Preparing for Tax Filings

Preparation for tax filings involves meticulous organization of financial records, ensuring all necessary documents and information are readily available for tax reporting. This includes income statements, balance sheets, expense records, receipts, and any other relevant financial documentation.

Proper tax planning throughout the year facilitates smooth tax filings. By maintaining accurate records and staying informed about tax law changes, businesses can optimize deductions, credits, and exemptions, ultimately minimizing tax liabilities while ensuring compliance with regulatory requirements

ADVANCED FEATURES AND INTEGRATIONS

5.1 Integrating Third-Party Apps with QuickBooks Online

Integrating third-party apps with QuickBooks Online (QBO) offers businesses a seamless way to enhance their accounting processes. The QuickBooks App Store serves as a hub for various apps that cater to different business needs. From inventory management to CRM tools, businesses can explore a plethora of applications tailored to complement QBO's functionalities. **Exploring the QuickBooks App Store** is a fundamental step in understanding the diverse array of options available.

The process of **Connecting E-commerce Platforms** to QuickBooks Online is vital for businesses engaging in online sales. By integrating platforms like Shopify, WooCommerce, or BigCommerce with QBO, businesses can synchronize sales data, track inventory, and manage finances more efficiently. This integration streamlines operations, reducing manual entry and minimizing errors.

Streamlining Business Operations with Integrations

involves more than just connecting apps. It's about optimizing workflows and creating synergies between different software solutions. For instance, integrating time-tracking apps like TSheets or scheduling tools like Calendly with QuickBooks Online can enhance efficiency by automating data entry, saving time, and ensuring accuracy.

5.2 Automating Recurring Transactions

Setting up **Recurring Invoices** in QuickBooks Online simplifies billing for businesses with regular clients. Automating these invoices saves time and ensures timely payments. Businesses can set up recurring schedules based on specific dates or intervals, allowing for customized billing cycles.

Automating **Bill Payments** is another essential aspect of transaction automation. By linking vendors to bills and setting up automatic payments, businesses can save time and reduce the risk of missing payment deadlines. This process involves scheduling payments based on due dates or specific parameters, enabling better cash flow management.

Implementing **Time-Saving Tips for Transaction Automation** involves optimizing recurring transaction setups. It includes regularly reviewing and updating recurring transactions to accommodate changes in payment amounts, frequencies, or billing details. Additionally, ensuring that all transactions are accurately categorized and reconciled contributes to smoother financial operations.

5.3 Multi-Currency Transactions

Enabling **Multi-Currency Features** in QuickBooks Online allows businesses to transact in various currencies. This feature is crucial for companies engaging in international trade. It enables the creation of invoices, tracking expenses, and receiving payments in multiple currencies, streamlining global transactions.

Managing **Exchange Rates** is essential in multi-currency environments. QuickBooks Online updates exchange rates automatically, but businesses may also need to manually adjust rates based on market fluctuations. Understanding how to manage and update exchange rates ensures accurate financial reporting.

Handling **Foreign Transactions** involves accounting for gains or losses due to currency fluctuations. QuickBooks Online provides tools to handle gains/losses arising from currency exchange, allowing businesses to track these fluctuations and maintain accurate financial records.

5.4 Customizing and Scaling QuickBooks Online

Personalizing Forms and Templates in QuickBooks Online allows businesses to create a professional and branded look for their documents. By customizing invoices, estimates, and reports with company logos, colors, and fonts, businesses can reinforce their brand identity.

Adding Custom Fields and Labels to QuickBooks Online provides flexibility in capturing additional business-specific information. Custom fields allow users to input unique data relevant to their operations, enhancing reporting and tracking capabilities beyond standard fields.

Scaling QuickBooks for Business Growth involves optimizing workflows, considering system integrations, and ensuring the software accommodates the increasing complexity and volume of business transactions. This includes regularly assessing the need for additional features, users, or advanced functionalities to align with evolving business requirements.

TROUBLESHOOTING AND FAQS

5.1 Integrating Third-Party Apps with QuickBooks Online

Integrating third-party apps with QuickBooks Online (QBO) offers businesses a seamless way to enhance their accounting processes. The QuickBooks App Store serves as a hub for various apps that cater to different business needs. From inventory management to CRM tools, businesses can explore a plethora of applications tailored to complement QBO's functionalities. **Exploring the QuickBooks App Store** is a fundamental step in understanding the diverse array of options available.

The process of **Connecting E-commerce Platforms** to QuickBooks Online is vital for businesses engaging in online sales. By integrating platforms like Shopify, WooCommerce, or BigCommerce with QBO, businesses can synchronize sales data, track inventory, and manage finances more efficiently. This integration streamlines operations, reducing manual entry and minimizing errors.

Streamlining Business Operations with Integrations

involves more than just connecting apps. It's about optimizing workflows and creating synergies between different software solutions. For instance, integrating time-tracking apps like TSheets or scheduling tools like Calendly with QuickBooks Online can enhance efficiency by automating data entry, saving time, and ensuring accuracy.

5.2 Automating Recurring Transactions

Setting up **Recurring Invoices** in QuickBooks Online simplifies billing for businesses with regular clients. Automating these invoices saves time and ensures timely payments. Businesses can set up recurring schedules based on specific dates or intervals, allowing for customized billing cycles.

Automating **Bill Payments** is another essential aspect of transaction automation. By linking vendors to bills and setting up automatic payments, businesses can save time and reduce the risk of missing payment deadlines. This process involves scheduling payments based on due dates or specific parameters, enabling better cash flow management.

Implementing **Time-Saving Tips for Transaction Automation** involves optimizing recurring transaction setups. It includes regularly reviewing and updating recurring transactions to accommodate changes in payment amounts, frequencies, or billing details. Additionally, ensuring that all transactions are accurately categorized and reconciled contributes to smoother financial operations.

5.3 Multi-Currency Transactions

Enabling **Multi-Currency Features** in QuickBooks Online

allows businesses to transact in various currencies. This feature is crucial for companies engaging in international trade. It enables the creation of invoices, tracking expenses, and receiving payments in multiple currencies, streamlining global transactions.

Managing **Exchange Rates** is essential in multi-currency environments. QuickBooks Online updates exchange rates automatically, but businesses may also need to manually adjust rates based on market fluctuations. Understanding how to manage and update exchange rates ensures accurate financial reporting.

Handling **Foreign Transactions** involves accounting for gains or losses due to currency fluctuations. QuickBooks Online provides tools to handle gains/losses arising from currency exchange, allowing businesses to track these fluctuations and maintain accurate financial records.

5.4 Customizing and Scaling QuickBooks Online

Personalizing Forms and Templates in QuickBooks Online allows businesses to create a professional and branded look for their documents. By customizing invoices, estimates, and reports with company logos, colors, and fonts, businesses can reinforce their brand identity.

Adding Custom Fields and Labels to QuickBooks Online provides flexibility in capturing additional business-specific information. Custom fields allow users to input unique data relevant to their operations, enhancing reporting and tracking capabilities beyond standard fields.

Scaling QuickBooks for Business Growth involves optimizing workflows, considering system integrations, and ensuring the software accommodates the increasing complexity and volume of business transactions. This includes regularly assessing the need for additional features, users, or advanced functionalities to align with evolving business requirements.

COMMON QUICKBOOKS ONLINE ISSUES AND SOLUTIONS

QuickBooks Online, despite its efficiency, occasionally encounters various issues that can disrupt workflow. **Login and Accessibility Problems** are among the most common. These issues may arise due to internet connectivity, browser cache, or login credential errors. Troubleshooting involves clearing cache and cookies, ensuring stable internet connectivity, and verifying login credentials. In cases of forgotten passwords, following the password recovery process is essential.

Error Messages and Notifications within QuickBooks Online can be perplexing and interrupt regular operations. They range from generic errors to specific issues related to data import, transactions, or software updates. Each error message requires a tailored approach for resolution. Understanding the error code and researching solutions through QuickBooks' knowledge base or community forums can often provide valuable insights into resolving these issues.

Troubleshooting Sync Issues is crucial, especially for businesses utilizing multiple devices or integrating third-party applications with QuickBooks Online. Sync errors may stem from connectivity problems or conflicts between different software versions. Resolving these involves checking internet connectivity, updating software, ensuring compatibility between integrated applications, and verifying sync settings within QuickBooks Online.

6.2 Best Practices for Data Accuracy

Maintaining **Regular Data Backups** is fundamental for data integrity and security. QuickBooks Online provides backup functionalities, allowing users to safeguard their financial data. Scheduled backups, either through the internal backup system or external cloud services, ensure that data remains safe and retrievable in case of unexpected system failures or data loss incidents.

Auditing and Reconciling Accounts on a consistent basis ensures that financial records align accurately with bank statements and actual transactions. Reconciliations help identify discrepancies, prevent fraud, and maintain the accuracy and reliability of financial information within QuickBooks Online. Regular auditing ensures that the books remain up-to-date and reflect the true financial status of the business.

Performing **Data Cleanup and Maintenance** is essential for optimizing QuickBooks Online's performance. Over time, databases can accumulate redundant or obsolete information, leading to slower system performance. Regularly cleaning up outdated transactions, removing duplicate entries, and archiving old records streamlines the system, enhances efficiency, and prevents potential errors in financial reporting.

6.3 Frequently Asked Questions (FAQs)

Navigating **Support Resources** is crucial for QuickBooks Online users facing queries or issues. Understanding where to find help within the software, accessing official documentation, tutorials, or contacting customer support can significantly reduce troubleshooting time. Utilizing the Help section within QuickBooks Online and exploring the official website's support pages aids in finding quick solutions to common queries.

QuickBooks Online users often seek **Quick Solutions to Common Inquiries**. Frequently asked questions range from how-to queries about specific features to troubleshooting common errors. Providing concise and accurate answers to these queries, either through official support channels, community forums, or user-generated content, ensures users can swiftly resolve issues without extensive searching or waiting for support.

Engaging in **Community Forums and User Support** can be immensely beneficial for QuickBooks Online users. These forums serve as platforms where users share experiences, exchange knowledge, and offer solutions to various issues they've encountered. Engaging with the community allows users to learn from others' experiences, access diverse perspectives, and often find innovative solutions beyond official support channels

COLLABORATION AND MULTI-USER MANAGEMENT

7.1 Multi-User Collaboration in QuickBooks Online

QuickBooks Online offers a robust framework for multi-user collaboration, allowing businesses to set up a collaborative environment seamlessly. Setting up multiple users within QuickBooks Online involves several steps. Firstly, an administrator or the primary user needs to navigate to the 'Manage Users' section within the settings. Here, they can invite other team members by entering their email addresses and assigning appropriate roles.

7.1.1 Setting Up Multiple Users

The process of adding users typically involves defining permissions and access levels for each individual. QuickBooks provides various user roles such as 'Company Administrator,' 'Standard User,' 'Reports Only,' and more, each with different privileges and restrictions. For instance, a Company Administrator has access to all features and settings, while a Reports Only user can only view financial reports. This setup ensures that team members have tailored access according to their responsibilities, enhancing security and efficiency.

7.1.2 User Permissions and Access Controls

User permissions and access controls play a pivotal role in maintaining data integrity and security. It's crucial to configure permissions accurately to prevent unauthorized access to sensitive financial information. For instance, restricting access to financial transactions or sensitive reports can prevent accidental modifications or data breaches. QuickBooks Online's granular permission settings allow businesses to customize access rights for various modules and functions, striking a balance between collaboration and security.

7.1.3 Managing Collaborative Workflows

Efficient management of collaborative workflows within QuickBooks Online hinges on clear communication and streamlined processes. Users can collaborate on transactions, invoices, and reports in real-time, fostering a cohesive work environment. Utilizing features like the 'Notes' section on transactions allows team members to leave comments or instructions, facilitating smoother collaboration. Additionally, assigning specific tasks or responsibilities within QuickBooks simplifies tracking progress and ensuring accountability among team members.

7.2 Integrating Team Communication Tools

Integrating QuickBooks Online with various team communication platforms enhances connectivity and collaboration within finance teams. Seamless integration enables users to bridge the gap between financial data and team discussions, facilitating informed decision-making.

7.2.1 Connecting QuickBooks with Communication Platforms

Integration with communication tools like Slack, Microsoft Teams, or other platforms allows team members to receive real-time notifications or updates regarding financial transactions, invoices, or pending approvals directly within their communication channels. This integration streamlines communication by centralizing discussions around financial data, reducing the need for constant context switching between tools.

7.2.2 Streamlining Communication for Finance Teams

Finance teams often handle critical information, and effective communication is paramount. Integration of communication tools with QuickBooks Online enables swift communication regarding financial queries, approvals, or discrepancies. Teams can collaborate on specific transactions or financial reports within their preferred communication platform, fostering a transparent and efficient workflow.

7.2.3 Improving Collaboration Efficiency

By integrating communication tools, QuickBooks Online not only facilitates communication but also improves collaboration efficiency. Real-time discussions, quick decision-making, and immediate responses to financial queries result in a more agile and responsive finance team. Moreover, the ability to attach files or links directly from QuickBooks within communication threads reduces the chance of errors or misinterpretation, enhancing overall collaboration quality.

7.3 Audit Trails and Security Measures

Maintaining a secure environment and ensuring the

integrity of financial data is crucial for businesses using QuickBooks Online. Audit trails and security measures play a pivotal role in achieving this goal.

7.3.1 Tracking Changes and User Activities

Audit trails in QuickBooks Online record every change made to financial data, providing a comprehensive history of transactions, modifications, and user activities. This detailed log allows administrators or auditors to track changes, identify discrepancies, and maintain accountability within the system. Accessing and reviewing these logs can help pinpoint errors or unauthorized actions, ensuring data accuracy and reliability.

7.3.2 Implementing Two-Factor Authentication

Enhancing security measures within QuickBooks Online includes implementing two-factor authentication (2FA). This additional layer of security requires users to provide a second form of verification, typically a code sent to their mobile device or email, along with their login credentials. 2FA significantly reduces the risk of unauthorized access, adding an extra barrier against potential threats like phishing or credential theft.

7.3.3 Ensuring Data Security and Compliance

QuickBooks Online prioritizes data security and compliance with various industry standards. Encrypted connections, secure data storage, and regular system updates contribute to safeguarding sensitive financial information. Furthermore, compliance features cater to specific regulatory requirements, ensuring that businesses adhere to standards like GDPR, HIPAA, or others applicable to their industry. Regular security audits and prompt action on potential vulnerabilities strengthen the platform's resilience against evolving threats.

This comprehensive approach to multi-user collaboration, integration with communication tools, and robust security measures within QuickBooks Online empowers businesses to streamline workflows, enhance collaboration, and safeguard sensitive financial data effectively.

MOBILE ACCOUNTING WITH QUICKBOOKS ONLINE

8.1 Accessing QuickBooks Online from Mobile Devices

8.1.1 Downloading and Installing the Mobile App

Accessing QuickBooks Online via mobile devices has become increasingly convenient with the dedicated mobile app. To start, users can download the QuickBooks Online mobile app from the respective app store based on their device's operating system (iOS or Android). Once downloaded, follow the installation prompts, granting necessary permissions. The installation process is relatively straightforward, mirroring the user-friendly approach QuickBooks is known for.

8.1.2 Logging In and Syncing Data

Upon installation, users are required to log in using their

existing QuickBooks Online credentials. This step ensures data synchronization between the mobile app and the web version, providing seamless access to financial records, transactions, and reports across devices. The login process is secure and may require additional verification steps for enhanced security, such as two-factor authentication.

8.1.3 Mobile Features and Limitations

The QuickBooks Online mobile app offers a range of features tailored for on-the-go accounting management. Users can access customer information, create and send invoices, manage expenses, and categorize transactions directly from their mobile devices. However, while the app provides substantial functionalities, certain features available on the web platform might have limitations or different interfaces on mobile. Users might experience some constraints when dealing with complex financial tasks or detailed reporting, prompting the need to switch to the desktop version for comprehensive functionality.

8.2 Managing Transactions On The Go

8.2.1 Creating Invoices and Expenses

One of the significant advantages of accessing QuickBooks Online via mobile devices is the ability to create and send invoices or record expenses instantly. The user-friendly interface allows for quick entry of invoice details, including client information, services/products rendered, payment terms, and due dates. Likewise, expense tracking becomes efficient by snapping photos of receipts, which can be instantly logged into the system, reducing manual data entry.

8.2.2 Capturing Receipts with Mobile Devices

The mobile app's functionality extends to capturing and digitizing receipts, eliminating the hassle of managing paper documents. Users can simply take pictures of receipts using their mobile devices and attach them directly to corresponding transactions within QuickBooks Online. This feature not only streamlines expense tracking but also ensures a paperless approach to maintaining financial records, enhancing organization and accessibility.

8.2.3 Real-Time Updates and Notifications

Managing transactions on the go via QuickBooks Online provides real-time updates and notifications. Users receive immediate alerts on payment receipts, invoice views, or overdue payments, enabling swift action and better control over cash flow management. These real-time updates empower users to stay informed and promptly address any financial matters, contributing to efficient business operations.

8.3 Mobile Reporting And Analytics

8.3.1 Viewing Financial Reports on Mobile

QuickBooks Online facilitates the viewing of essential financial reports directly on mobile devices. Users can access balance sheets, profit and loss statements, cash flow reports, and more, allowing for quick assessments of the business's financial health. However, the complexity of detailed or customized reports might present limitations on mobile screens, suggesting a more comprehensive analysis through the web version for intricate reporting needs.

8.3.2 Analyzing KPIs and Performance Metrics

The mobile reporting feature includes the ability to analyze key performance indicators (KPIs) and crucial business metrics. While users can access summarized data and trends, in-depth analysis might be better suited for the desktop version due to the mobile interface's limitations. Nonetheless, the mobile reporting functionality empowers users with instant insights into business performance, enabling quick decision-making on the move.

8.3.3 Tracking Business Insights Anywhere

The convenience of mobile reporting extends to tracking business insights from anywhere with internet access. This feature enables business owners and managers to stay updated on critical financial information while away from the office. The accessibility to essential reports and insights on mobile devices enhances flexibility and responsiveness in decision-making, contributing to more agile business operations

CONCLUSION

9.1 Small Business Success with QuickBooks Online

Navigating the intricacies of small business management has been significantly aided by the utilization of QuickBooks Online. This cloud-based accounting software has proven instrumental in streamlining operations, enabling businesses to scale efficiently. Examining specific case studies sheds light on the transformative impact QuickBooks Online has had on various sectors.

9.1.1 Case Study: Retail Business Transformation

Consider the case of a small retail business that transitioned to QuickBooks Online. By leveraging its robust features, the business enhanced inventory management, streamlined sales tracking, and optimized cash flow. Real-time insights into sales trends and inventory turnover empowered the business to make informed decisions, resulting in improved profitability and operational efficiency.

9.1.2 Success Story: Service Industry Optimization

Another success story lies in the service industry, where a company integrated QuickBooks Online into its operations. By utilizing the software's invoicing capabilities and expense tracking functionalities, this service-based business streamlined client billing and monitored expenditures more effectively. The accessibility of financial data facilitated budgeting and resource allocation, ultimately contributing to increased client satisfaction and revenue growth.

9.1.3 Lessons Learned from Real-Life Implementations

These real-life implementations highlight valuable lessons for small businesses adopting QuickBooks Online. Firstly, customization is key—tailoring the software to specific business needs enhances its effectiveness. Secondly, consistent utilization and proper training across the team ensure maximum utilization of the software's capabilities. Lastly, ongoing support and staying updated with new features and updates are crucial for continued success.

9.2 Overcoming Challenges with QuickBooks Online

Amidst the business landscape's dynamic challenges, QuickBooks Online has emerged as an invaluable tool for resilience and adaptation. Examining real-world scenarios showcases its role in overcoming hurdles and navigating through unforeseen difficulties.

9.2.1 Case Study: Navigating Financial Crisis

In the face of a financial crisis, a company utilizing QuickBooks Online found itself equipped to weather the storm. The software's real-time financial tracking capabilities enabled swift decision-making, allowing the business to identify areas for cost reduction, manage cash flow more effectively, and access crucial financial reports promptly. This enabled the business to mitigate the impacts of the crisis and emerge more resilient.

9.2.2 Success Story: Adapting to Market Changes

Another instance involves a business that swiftly adapted to market changes with QuickBooks Online.

The software's flexibility allowed for quick adjustments in pricing strategies, expense management, and resource allocation. By leveraging the platform's insights, the business navigated market shifts, adapted its services to meet evolving customer demands, and maintained competitiveness in a rapidly changing landscape.

9.2.3 Strategies for Overcoming Common Challenges

These case studies underscore strategies for businesses facing challenges. Firstly, proactive financial planning and monitoring through QuickBooks Online aid in identifying potential risks and opportunities. Secondly, embracing agility and flexibility in response to market changes enhances adaptability. Lastly, leveraging the software's capabilities to streamline operations ensures a robust foundation for overcoming adversities.

9.3 Best Practices from QuickBooks Online Users

Drawing from the experiences of proficient QuickBooks Online users reveals key practices that contribute to efficient financial management and maximize the software's benefits.

9.3.1 Tips for Efficient Financial Management

Efficient financial management involves regular reconciliation of accounts, categorizing transactions accurately, and utilizing reports for informed decision-making. Furthermore, maintaining organized records, utilizing invoicing features effectively, and staying updated with tax regulations are crucial aspects that contribute to smooth financial operations.

9.3.2 Implementing Time-Saving Workflows

Leveraging automation features within QuickBooks

Online can significantly save time. Setting up recurring transactions, automating bill payments, and utilizing bank feeds for real-time data entry streamline processes and minimize manual input, allowing businesses to focus on core activities.

9.3.3 Insights for Maximizing QuickBooks Online Benefits

Maximizing QuickBooks Online benefits involves exploring the platform's integrations with other business tools, seeking continuous learning opportunities through available resources, and engaging with the QuickBooks community for insights, tips, and best practices. Regularly evaluating and optimizing the use of features aligns the software with evolving business needs, ensuring maximum efficiency and effectiveness.